Trailing The Sun's Sweat

Poetry by
Jacqueline de Weever

THE POET'S PRESS
Pittsburgh, PA

Copyright © 2015 by Jacqueline de Weever
All Rights Reserved
Second printing, 2017

Grateful acknowledgement is made to the following journals in which these poems, some in slightly different form, have appeared:

California Quarterly — "Geography Lessons"
Edgz — "Cosmography"
(formerly "Cosmography: The Maya Weaver")
Homestead Review — "Nomads"
NYCBigCityLit.com — "Maps"
Sensations Magazine — "Noose"
(formerly "Elegy for Jacqueline Peters") and
"Tituba: Flame Skimmer"
(formerly "Tibuba's Defiance: Andean Gift")
Ship of Fools — "Mirage of Cipangu"
Tribeca Review — "Cross Pollination"

ISBN 0-922558-77-9

This is the 210th publication of
THE POET'S PRESS
2209 MURRAY AVENUE #3
PITTSBURGH, PA 15217
www.poetspress.org

For Sam and Dick and for Woodstock

CONTENTS

Trailing the Sun's Sweat   *9*
Forced March   *13*
Pond Hawk (1492)   *14*
Rites for Wanderers   *16*
Orb-Weaving Spider   *17*
Early Whispers   *18*
Fragrant Land   *19*
Mirage of Cipangu   *21*
Lament   *23*
Cento: Siren Songs   *24*
Darning Needles   *25*
Firefly Dances   *26*
Meadow Hawk (1616)   *27*
Otherworld Ambush   *28*
Explorer's Map   *29*
Maps   *31*
Traces   *32*
Zong Survivor's Psalm (1781)   *33*
Songs from a Spider   *34*
Tituba: Flame Skimmer   *35*
Noose   *36*
Sacrifice   *37*
Andean Song   *39*
Sea Creatures   *40*
Sugar's Trap   *41*
Ticuna Response   *42*
Currency   *43*

WHO WINS?

Self-Portrait 47
Geography Lessons 48
The Craft of Erasure 49
Cross Pollination 50
Nomads 51
Ceremonial Ode 52
Winter Solstice 53
Rarities 54
Wandering Glider 55
Ghost Songs 56
Leaf, Vine, Fruit 57
Dislocation 58
New Year's Eve 59
Sacred Landscape 60
Communing with the Dead 62
Caimans Crossing 63
Sea Cucumbers 64
The Hidden God 65
Minus a Goddess 66
Morpho Trail 67
Night-Blooming Cereus 69
Victory 70
Secret Texts 71
Dolphin Dances 72
Celebration 73

ABOUT THE POEMS 75

ABOUT THE AUTHOR 78

ABOUT THIS BOOK 79

Inca terms:
> gold: sweat of the sun
> silver: tears of the moon

Trailing the Sun's Sweat

Before he rises from desire's delights
he embraces earth's folds
his sweat lodged in her crevices
like spice a lover leaves
in the sheets.

Earth rolls over; the sweat congeals
an aphrodisiac so potent
it stirs lust in men's blood.
And they follow like dogs
to claw Sun's gift
from earth's breast.

What do I give my heart to?
Softer ravishment:
the river's sunlit cap on the tide's way out,
algae living on sun's streaks
his reflection in the moon's tears
setting campfires to light
tracks left in a trail of stars.

Trailing the Sun's Sweat

FORCED MARCH

Which leaf, what plant or flower packed
in parchment by botanists companioning
slave-ferries of humans wedged in excrement

can erase shackle bruises healed
to ridges of jelled skin?

Swept along by winds
wild mustard flourishes
everywhere.

I discover blossoms from Bombay
vegetables from Nigeria
trophies flaunted by English Kew,

snatched from afar:
the giant water-lily Yrupe,
rope-root anchors of my childhood.

Crab grass flowers through lemongrass
bamboo invades and conquers
colonials in my ancestral garden.

Chinese hibiscus and hydrangea flourish
lost to origin; nymphs of the pond
remember Egypt, dare to bloom West.

My clippers prune the *frangipani*.
Aztec *cacalo*, temple flower
for the dead.

POND HAWK (1492)

Banners of Castile and Leon flash
over the Alhambra; Jews, Moors
and Saracens driven across the Middle Sea.

Now for the Grand Khan, Cathay
beyond the Canaries whose scent of sugar
tickled his nostrils on his way to Guinea.

Trade winds dizzy his sails
or freeze them becalmed.
Not now hurricanes to hang
fish in trees.

He doesn't know that his compass
spinning north-west north-east
is a meteor shower plunging his world
into turbulence.

Entangled in sweet ripening greed for gold
he wanders emerald-sapphire seas.
Islands suddenly puncture the horizon.

Not now earth-gobbles
of palm trees, people.

Special cargo — viruses of death.
Red tarantulas large as crabs
lurk in the forest mold.

Crowns of Castile and Leon flutter over
Xamaica, Guanahani
signal to pirate sharks, fins breaking paths
for Jews,
Saracens,
Moors.

RITES FOR WANDERERS

Root a prayer stick, cotton thread,
notched with corn flowers

sacred to peoples forced to wander
vagrants in search of home,

seeking gardens and pastures
lost in prairie and savannah

hearts soaring from ponds
like body's dragonflies.

Rise from the lake
dance over water,
scoop sunshine

snatch rain from clouds
to swell maize,
flood the rice fields.

Hover here before
the next fly over.

ORB-WEAVING SPIDER

She huddles at its center
as the moon rides the clouds
spittle silk churned from her belly
trap for beetle, firefly, wasp

testing suspension
between dust-crusted limbs
of an old frangipani
crowded with blooms:

an ancient art of entrapment.

Precision launch
from center to twig
shuttle back to web's navel,
out again in the night dew.

Green lacewings tangle
as embroidery, sphinx moths
flutter in her threads.

Day unravels what
night has woven —

another night a new web
to form a tapestry
of riddles.

EARLY WHISPERS

What water birds are these,
   giant egrets floating off our coast?

Men walk on their backs.
Are they creatures from sea caves?
Or like Arawaks, from the sky?
        Perhaps raptors, ready to tear open
soft bellies of our islands,
penetrate our forests,
slice our drums.

Parrots swoop by floated by wind gusts;
the sky vertigo blue obscures
the coming hurricane's fury.

Shall we restring our songs?
First, our customs for friends
              — fruit, a gold mask —
Then —
              sharpen our shell arrow points.

Or will we leave shadows carved
on pebbles
bordering seaweed?

FRAGRANT LAND

*The breezes were softer than in April at Seville;...
They are so laden in scent.* — Christopher Columbus, *Journal*

Scents from fruit, leaves, bark
steal into his sails.
The forest sees.
Sun, too brilliant, casts dark shadows
on its floor alive with poison centipedes.

Bush dawn blushes the east.
Westward, night retreats, the waning moon
a sickle on its back.
Faces colored nutmeg, apricot
under paint from black plums
appear; naked bodies bearing long black hair,
women wear small cotton aprons.

One man's gold nose-ring sparks
his desire; another wears a band on his arm,
still another a bracelet on his leg.
Where does it come from?

For now, a flood of marigolds
yellow birds' song,
coos and wing whispers in the leaves;
in the distance, a river wanders
through the trees' branches.

Jolting awake, he trades hawks' bells
trainer of sparrow-hawks,
precision hunters
of small birds.

MIRAGE OF CIPANGU

I wish to leave for another very large island.
Which I believe must be Cipangu. — C. Columbus, *Journal*

Guanahani:
first gamble succeeds; very green land, breezes soft,
the Bahamas unleash their magic of fragrance and form,
I don't want to lose time; I must make the island
of Cipangu.

Colba:
flocks of parrots blot the sun;
their harsh calls compel a pause to listen;
this is not Cipangu with pearls, gold, spices.

Baneque:
so rich no need to work for food and clothing,
trees bearing cotton to net his feet. But where's the gold?
I do nothing but go forward to find gold.

Guarione:
Cacique Guacanagari gifts him a mask of beaten gold.
Its craft dazzles, but where is it gathered?
I took the natives by force to give me information.

Fruit trees
full of birdsong delay him for two hours; their narcotic of scents
assail the nostrils, but lust for gold his antidote and bond.
  I do nothing but go forward hoping to find gold.

"Witch"
I cry out "halt the journey," the islands' spells must tie
his feet to the ground, must quench obsession.
  I do not wish to delay in finding gold.

LAMENT

All display the most extraordinarily gentle behavior.
— C. Columbus, *Journal.*

They were too gentle to make a sweep
    of your men setting foot on their beach of sand.
You plot their enslavement and I weep
    that their offers of cassava and casareep
did not contrive the magic wand
    of their safety, far too gentle to sweep
away bribes of green beads, hawks' bells, cheap
    exchange for gold masks, given open-hand.
Instead their enslavement, and I weep
    because you saw gold floating on the deep
as the river flows; you will demand
    that these gentle people begin to sweep
those rivers, to gather and heap
    gold into hawks' bells free of the sand
waiting to shroud them as slaves, and I weep
    that their welcome could not leap
beyond your lust, to interlace strands
    of their lives in a gentle sweep
to escape enslavement and I weep.

CENTO: SIREN SONGS

*The singing of little birds is such that . . .
a man could never wish to leave this place.*
— C. Columbus, *Journal*

The nightingale was singing.
Yellow Warbler's my name. You left him at home
    in Saragossa.

There were many . . . small birds which sang very sweetly,
Not mermaids, your hallucination.

*For . . . two hours I walked among trees, the loveliest sight
    I have ever seen.*
Silence under the ceiba tree.   I held my song, watching...

So great a joy to hear the singing of the birds.
Not babblers like the sea against your ship.

I could not weary of the songs of birds.
  We'll glue your feet among ground orchids.

*The chirping of the crickets went on all night
    at which all were delighted*
Those were ancient immortals haunting the trees.

It is a land to be desired and, when seen, never to be left.
Vultures follow, blacked by our dirges.

DARNING NEEDLES

The king sent him a great mask of gold.
— C. Columbus, *Journal*

Ceiba wood
overlaid with beaten gold —

Guacanagari smokes out
Columbus's craving
behind gestures of friendship.

Chief's gift from the tree of life:
stirs heat to run through
the visitor's veins.

Columbus gives a collar from his neck:
bloodstones, and a large silver ring
to spin a web of exchange.

Could gifts mend fabric
already torn
by the admiral's greed?

Chief understands;
commands secrecy;
Columbus hides his weapons
later-spouting fire.

FIREFLY DANCES

White wild orchids shroud
first peoples' dance imprints
from surface reading;

twill baskets capture frog and monkey
in designs to match the cosmos,
fade in water-ruin;
feather aprons fragment.

Instead, splinters of pot patterns,
fossilized wood from gardens
in remnants of camp
discards.

Who can capture footprints
of ceremonial dances?

No pyramid to mark conquest,
no temple tomb where immured wives
and slaves companion the netherworld.

And death?
Only bones gleam stark white,
once smeared with honey
for ants to demolish,

since when the dance ends
music of feet and flute
dissolves in the rush and flight
of scarlet macaws.

MEADOW HAWK (1616)

Wandering the meadows of England
I imitated a shepherd
wooing his mistress;
the hawk of my ambition
folded his wings.

Raleigh, explorer in my withered winter;
I circle, swoop on wilds
   of everlasting green among
new-found peoples painted faces, poisoned darts,
prey to the savage beak
gnawing my innards.

I crave Guiana's El Dorado,
wagering my life,
not for trade in Seville oranges
or like a vulture to take the forest's maidenhead
   the way Pizarro took Peru's.

I hold my soul in my teeth.
   to shape something new
from snake rivers swarming with caiman
waiting to swallow my men. Death's door opens
   after my third pursuit.

Heavy mists spume up on the *Destiny's* afterdeck,
   warm air colliding with changing winds
of the Horse Latitudes.
My haunting: block, sword, and basket
   to catch my sliced-off head.

OTHERWORLD AMBUSH

They rolled out of ships
impoverished young men
with cargo — guns, horses, dogs,
almighty smallpox,

fatal for forest dwellers in endless green
of thick vines, turgid rivers
hunting peccary and fish
arrows tipped with stone and curare.

Mother Amazon's defenses:
an arsenal of malaria and typhus
tucked into the anopheles mosquito.

I am the result,
speaking their languages,
with a Dutch name,
my eyes slanted,
gift from my Javanese great grandfather,

my umbilical cord
buried in the lotus-clogged marshes,
to which I shall return.

EXPLORER'S MAP

Its 17th-century Latin title shouts:

NOVA TOTIUS ORBIS TERRARUM TABULA
(New Map of the Whole Circle of Earth)

On Ortelius's map, Latin intrudes into worlds
it does not know:
from west edge of Africa
to east limit of North America

familiar world I prepare to remake
from three thousand tiny pieces.

Flourishing unknown to each other
peoples will now meet.

Beginnings: pretty little ships point west,
sails full-bellied; pregnant with cargoes
of catastrophe —
                humans, dogs, horses —
to terrify the people;

fired weapons to flame gods, flutes, bark cloth,
                — home to poems and rites —
dying ashes to mingle with camp fires
soon washed into black rivers.

Did Ortelius, explorer by map, know
this world forged by ships controlled
by ghost-fathers?
                      Their descendants claim
the right to carry death in their pockets.

MAPS

Spaces on old maps ———
     blank   because the explorer
couldn't imagine people
who live in such spaces.
                What they coveted
holds my histories,
built of several ancestries.

Ah! Spur for land cloaked
as knowledge!
Possibilities, spiced by greed.
Spaces left blank
could not assign a place
for a creature not the three-toed sloth,
     even Lake Parima,
with a magical beast,
under the binoculars
yielded only water.

Yet the old map, tinted with
my shape to come,   hidden there,
with scarlet of macaws or red ibis,
         in the black abyss,
my ancestors haunting the cliff of my cheekbone
     like swift waters over
a waterfall's rock-face. There I live
        not tracked on explorers' maps.

TRACES

Columbus spoke no Arawak;
he understood Taino offers
of pineapple, cassava bread.

Thick leaves, heavy vines,
trunks several meters wide
block the paths to villages
whose fires light dances telling stories,
bone flutes carry heart beats
to disappear in camp smoke.

My words — cookie, caucus, skip —
spark the lightning bolt that cracks the jar
of loves pickled in vinegar of past grabfests,
a mix of Dutch, Algonquian, English,
with bitter aftertaste and tingling scent.

Relics.
Taino deaths beasts gods forest-rites
irrupt from their unmarked graves.
When I collect the broken glass
of their mourning songs, wounds
open in my naked hands.

ZONG SURVIVOR'S PSALM (1781)

Jamaica,
and light blinds me after the dark
of the slaver *Zong*,
my black body exposed for inspection.
Buyers measure my chest for strength,
my genitals for the perfection of horses.

Dizzy,
I hear the shrieks of my fellows
shackled, dumped overboard
to save drinking water
for whites who might die
for lack of it.

Sharks splash against the ship,
eager for Africans, helpless.
against traders expert
in work of
kidnap,
collar,
sell
store like spoons, head to toe,
cargo alive

which I am, now,
in the sun's ferocity.
I swear my life
in an alien world
to the sorcery of vultures
on the market's roof.

SONGS FROM A SPIDER

Spider Ananci, story-weaver in the Bight of Benin,
hitches a ride on a sardined African
crosses the Atlantic to an empire of sugar, lash, pain,

where flower songs tell of flight
from plaza to forest.

Yoruba stories grafted to Aztec stems
exchange lion's mane for ocelot's black roses,
black-and-white moths of Guinea
for the Amazon's dense blue morphos.

Ananci wraps his new coat
of hummingbird feathers close
magenta, indigo, orange;

his web of stories and songs
stronger than the obsidian knife
of the butterfly goddess
used in sacrifice

and everywhere flame-trees and flame-vines
shouting to African caryatids
of the barbarian empire

fire the remedy.

TITUBA: FLAME SKIMMER

Branded witch
threatened with pitch
fire can't frighten me,
        myself   fire   air   water   earth,

Shift of shape
signals escape
easy switch from woman to worm
to crocodile under lotus floats
        in root-tangled rivers.

I, Tituba,
fed them, healed
them, doors unsealed
with balsam, ginger, herbs and spices,
called back their dead with goat sacrifices.

My tribulation
is recognition
of their other shape, human as snake,
deceit their element as fire mine.

Sunset's amber:
time to meander.
        Flying foxes my companions
I ride their boom, skim the flames.

Witch.   Sorcerer.   Life.

NOOSE

(For Jacqueline Peters, Indian lynched by the Klan in 1981)

In olive grove the slender corpse sways
  in a cloud and odor of black flies' wings,
hate stamped in the welts her wounds raise.
  The olive grove would have shocked and dismayed
her when she set out that pleasant spring.
  Now the olives sleep as her slender corpse sways.
The flies eat at her mouth, half-crazed.
  Modern times, and a woman swings,
wrestles hate with the welts her wounds raise.
  The summer shirt loose at her throat is amazed
that it can't hide the blood that round her neck clings
  as a sleep of olives her slender corpse sways.
The Ku Klux Klan fully planned this crazed
  swing in the orchard. Yet the silence sings,
wrestles hate with the welts her wounds raise.
  They had hoped to muffle any praise
with rope and make the body swing.
  Among the olives, her slender corpse sways,
"Wrestle hate," shout the welts her wounds raise.

SACRIFICE

Strangled for earth's fruits:
— corn — beans — flocks
of thick-fleeced alpaca.
White caps of snow present the past
as they heave up the body
of the young woman, sacrificed,
red blood to hold the sun in place.
now revealed your ragged face.

Alpaca return the wool,
provision for your fine wrap;
earth burned into pots, designs
snatched from bud and field;
feathered crown from bright birds
led you to your waiting gods,
life and death are interlaced,
sacrifice their inscribed place.

Embalmed and preserved by the cold,
what butterfly dreams filled your eyes
now eaten by the ice and snow?
Surely the fires of your heart
glowed bronze in your cheeks,
and the play of intellect flickered
across your brow as you faced
the priest-held knife uncased.

You watched the black mountains
swallow the sun, red-flecked orange,
as it bowled into the sea five
hundred years ago, now erased by snow.
You float into our present space
as your wrappings are unlaced.

ANDEAN SONG

Peruvian *El Condor Pasa* from pan pipes,
pulse from guitars, curl and spiral in the air
   an open guitar-case requests
tears in the throat or a few coins

four musicians, (mountain people from the altiplano)
depend on the passersby
   to stop and let the music
   coil around them
   or to shrug off magic.

Their long black hair in pony tail or slung across shoulders,
(once bedazzlement of Spanish sailors and soldiers)

adds to the spell they create, at home
                 among tomatoes, squash, potatoes, corn,
they gave to nourish the world

            now vibrating with ancient songs
            in Spanish lilt
and the vultures have flown by.

SEA CREATURES

Three hundred years under water,
spirits of drowned slaves roam reefs
of the Carib sea
arms seaweed and sea moss,
hair coral and sea anemone
stings in their petal-like
              tentacles.

When the full moon flings gleaming roads
over the waves, spirits ride dark and light
patterns cast by lanterns
swinging from masts of fishing vessels.
Vision dulled, guests on cruise ships have no idea:
the sea they enjoy shapes a vast tomb for millions
pitched overboard
                      sick, dead, alive.

The local fisherman has seen them on full tide,
nomads between islands
whispering lost languages in warm winds.
waiting for the cyclones of hurricane season
to howl their vengeance in the ocean's
              requiems.

SUGAR'S TRAP

Not known here before Columbus

but after the crack of pig-skin lash
scared rivers of flesh on black backs
swinging the sharp machete,
noon sun burnt into naked shoulders.

Night-rages of a fiery deity
a presence visible in offering
as loss of finger or hand,

green leaf-spears guard the sweet
hidden in yellow stalks.
Snakes wander between the canes.
The Demerara River runs black and silent
as molasses.

Cane-cutter in Florida
the man from our village comes home,
walks the moonless night.

Suddenly, his laugh fills the dark;
we know it's not a donkey
braying at midnight.

TICUNA RESPONSE

Come down to the river
see dragonflies skim
along the edge.
Among long grasses,
I watch motor boats
churn brown water to tie up
at a wooden landing.

Voices louder than the boat's
engine hope to find
a lost Eden because
they've destroyed their own.
They shove their small boxes
in our faces,
prefer us painted with vegetable juice.
My old mother in faded dress
dances slowly for a few pennies.

Strangers want the shaman's secrets
about herbs to heal their sickness.

How does picturing my poverty
cure their troubles?

I call on rapids' boiling foams
to barrier the village;
the anaconda too raises its head;
the caiman to slap river mud
with its flat tail; days of rain
to drench the forest.

CURRENCY

African trade beads — made in Venice near the Adriatic
mosaics of bound glass not found
    in Ghana or Malawi:

gold leaf swirled into clay worked like cream,
sunflower yellow, deep indigo,
    native to Ghana and Malawi

These designs diagram strip, whip, fired indelible,
but unknown or erased in markets
    far from Ghana and Malawi.

delivered across seas in trade for human beauties
from savannah and forest, from huts
    in Ghana and Malawi.

Their ghosts infect later landscapes, in wind howls,
in lightning flash and thunder crash familiar
    in Ghana and Malawi,

before the clasp fastens them to the pillar of a neck
they hiss in the gentle swing,
    far from Ghana and Malawi.

Who Wins?

SELF-PORTRAIT

(dialogue with Elytis)

Here I am
churned out of rivers, leaves dissolved in their beds;
alligator imprinted on my mind
    one eye on watch;

initiate into secrets of petroglyph caves,
    ancient scorings on their walls;
hoarding golden shower petals and allamandas
    if the tree spirits allow;
famished for green melons and white jasmine
    that remove heart rot
even when I am lost in the dove's mourning.

But now I open my hands
    fragrant with thyme
my hair with nutmeg,

barefoot I walk over the flamboyants
    dropped in the heat of flowering,

and always I open my hands to let fall
    white ginger in clouds of butterflies,

even when the sky splits
    and the rain crashes down like waterfalls;
always I open my hands
    with no other riches, no other riches.

Geography Lessons

Vermeer's geographer pauses. V-shaped compass
inert in his hand, he gazes, rapt, out the window
scattering light on papers
in warm amber hues.

Movement halted. Does he dream
of the places he does not know but charts?

The world's wealth invades his quiet:
Turkish rug pushed aside in a small hill;
Chinese lacquered table behind him;

high on a chest, a globe. Does it accent
the Indian Ocean? From the picture's frame
half a painted map peeks out

guide to traders in tulips for transplant
in Dutch gardens, to silks,
silver, and slaves for the Indies,

to my uncle Aloysius, hovering here,
incognito, geographer, like him, Dutch-named,
outside the man's imagining, to appear

centuries later, his black skin
bestowed by a slave shipped along routes
shown by the map on the wall.

He explodes, split open
by those charts and maps,
in worlds beyond this Vermeer room.

THE CRAFT OF ERASURE

(after Darwish)

Describe the bougainvillea?
No encyclopedia is any help.

Paper flower — local word but stable,
 could sing in simple language,
its Arawak unwritten   suppressed
by Bougainville's botanist spying out
strange shrubs, naming and erasing
with a Latin mask.

spectabilis: spectacular reward after drought?
Heavy flowering
peruviana: origin? Why not brasiliana?

What is its name?
An Indian familiar runs
through its stamens,
hides in a small white flower
nestled in giddy color.

I could use alphabetics of heat, light.
Better, a botanics of echoes,
as I am an echo
hidden in dyes
from my ancestors.

From dead empires
a meaningless label sucks
a native's soul.

CROSS POLLINATION

We were honey bee hosts
to your wasp species
sweetening your lives
with
island sugar
indian opium
African slaves
worker bees coerced for northerners,
controlled in our southern fields
when you laid your eggs
in our bodies as we soared
from plant to flower to tree.

Some died from the parasites; others thrived
while the occupying army of warrior insects
altered our 8-shaped dance patterns,
renamed our flowers with theirs
(Poinciana, Bougainvillea, Plumeria)
changed the pace of our hum and whir.

Eggs hatched from our hostage bodies
imprinted with new figure-8 dances;
flowers we pollinate vary from earlier blooms
with colors that win prizes
at the world's flower shows;
porous, we carry the blueprint
of patterns as we were before;
new shapes design the hive,
change the taste of our honey.

NOMADS

Argentinian, but look:
in Morocco heart-shaped leaves, paper-thin
purple, magenta, hang over a white fence;
in Sicily borders for gardens.

I, too, come from the South,
vibrate in several colors of kin, follow
flower's routes, drought-tolerant,
vagabonding for pasture in northern lands,

a hunter-gatherer gleaning where I can,
always temporary, in search of home.
I root in new soil, claim the brilliant hues
of bougainvillea, name-trace of a Frenchman

for southern bloom;
other surprises sprout
from human seeds.

CEREMONIAL ODE

Squash flowers wreath my head
yellow and white from zucchini and pumpkin.
I wander in search of my jaguar soul.

Green cabbage cap shields from sun,
cauldron of a thousand flames.
Can fire light the way to my jaguar soul?

Tamarind pods girdle my robe,
knock with the rhythm of my jaunty walk.
Will they point me the way to my jaguar soul?

Long grasses, dried, bend in the wake
of his paw prints near the river's mud.
Can they lead me to my jaguar soul?

Constellations and stars, night's blanket,
won't warm the chill from the jungle floor,
will never uncover the way to my jaguar soul.

The crescent moon is a just-lit lamp
in the dark smears over my vagabond path
as I stumble and search for my jaguar soul.

WINTER SOLSTICE

Tonight I am Maya
weaver of the cosmos and its gods
into my garments
my shawl, my blouse,
although not my genes
but who knows?
People wandered from Asia
to the Pacific
ancestored my great-grandfather
who peeps out of my cheekbones
and slanted eyes.
Vagabonds of wind and wave
came home to the southern land as well.
Their charts?
Sky, stars, moon, sun
their accuracy now stuns scientists
who think knowledge is theirs.
Today, the sun crosses the center
of the celestial equator.
(Did *you* imagine such a thing?
But they knew it would happen)
May your own sun center
your equilibrium.

RARITIES

Outside the Metropolitan Museum
black youngsters break dance
upward, backward,

smiles and frowns pumping blood
into feet seeking the home ground
beneath them, human dragonflies

mesmerizing tourists who toss
nickels and dimes
to grace their upturned hats.

Inside, Juan de Pareja,
the Met's five-million-steal
stares from the wooden frame
Africa and Spain stamped on his skin.

Velasquez's black slave
who never mixed paints
for black court dwarf or black acrobat
challenges me
with his dagger look.

Dancers and slave
twirl through barriers.
Vagabondage —

WANDERING GLIDER

A gypsy in the garden
Frangipani blooms on a gnarled old tree,

its muscles knotted under the bark
its night fragrance filching sleep.

I join my uprooted clan relative
without its witchery.

To Aztecs, *cacalo*, temple flower, luring sphinx moths
to its bowl dry of nectar where, trapped, they die;

snaring Spanish empire builders to tropic swamps
Italian Frangipani scenting gloves
as romance decoy.

King Louis's garden mania commands Plumier
to exchange monastery for Martinique.
Plumeria buries *cacalo* in Latin.

Question to origins?
Not in the Bible. A flower undermining faith?
But Plumier died on a trip.

My original name: Berber? Yoruba?
Javanese? Chinese?

Looking for you I wrap my arms
about the tree's trunk,
dig my toes under the hard roots.

GHOST SONGS

Sorrow-psalms from ashes in two continents:

Navajo bags forged from old blankets
woven on small frames in the desert,
now leather-bound,
whisper from hemp, clay, wool,
knotted fringes of prairie shawls
still alive to walk in beauty.

They sing the duet of Indian hands
and modern saleswoman —
alien to each other —
nudging together in a
Park Avenue store.

Credit cards will take them home
to those deaf to cadences from shawl
or beads; their chants remind me
that the sun warms their dead
in the plains, the pampas,

in paths winding below thick forest canopy
sheltering the caiman in the alluvial mud
who shouts:

I am immortal.

Leaf, Vine, Fruit

Broken magnolia branches cover the green daffodil shoots
piercing half-thawed ground — winter's shambles

but here the vine sprouts, clings to the trunk
swollen with juices to extend its tentacles.

What depth, older than the vine, do the roots
plunge to, gather nourishment?

Secrets: bones unmarked
long become dust.

White blossoms shed, the pear tree's leaf hangs young,
chartreuse before the deep green of summer.

Has it sucked up long-dried blood
of Indian and slave to feed the vine's leaf?

Fruit?
Perfectly round young buds of pear
slow growth to summer's perfection.

I want to mourn Indian and slave
but earth's power urges magnolia, vine, pear
mutating the buried virus.

DISLOCATION

Between grey and lavender clouds
the Boeing hovers in a cave-like density;
rain beats against the window glass,

then a trio of rainbows.

We float in three curves; light bends to left,
to right, holds us up from below,
between north and south,

as I drift between alphabets picked up
in northern flea markets; scripts
blurred with rice paddies

tangled in marigolds
decoding differences:

nightingale or yellow warbler,
Daffodil or hibiscus?
Woods or jungle?

I hover at thresholds between departure
and homecoming, a southern seabird
hovering on wind currents
longing for earth

and the guava's fragrance
in her hidden gardens.

NEW YEAR'S EVE

Bacalau's aromas offer taste delights:
salted cod, robed in capers, olives,
Sicilian whites, Tuscan reds,
sauces for pasta that bite the tongue.

The old year drags its baggage of joys
and pains toward midnight's dump;
our laughter holds promises folded
like paper flowers strung over new year's
floods.

But cod layers memories
not yet tied up and tossed.

Another time, another climate
— easy food for slaves,
shipped from cold north to hot south
in salt, twenty-four hours of soaking
to remove, days before cooked.

Delicious comes in a different buffet:
tiny appetizers of fish cakes, mixed with
ground peppers and onion, lightly fried,
pared with wine, yes, rum, vodka,
sucking layers of memory from salted cod.

SACRED LANDSCAPE

Winkle:
small village tucked behind rice paddies,
   not on any map but once a Crown estate,
people owned by the Crown.
George/William/Victoria wore crowns;
   gold from slavery filled their treasuries.
For slaves the flint-edged whip;
   for them, violins stringed for dancing;
for slaves pine-box houses, troolie palm roofs;
   for them, shelters of stone and marble.

For me, ten years old, August means
   a house nestled in a thicket of trees,
lemons spilling over the back verandah.
   Sometimes I hear fidgets around shutters
or bounces against brilliant green waves
   in the field; a scent of spice when gusts rustle
together two stunted sage shrubs.

I wander a field yearning toward water, distant;
   weeds rush forward, snatch at red-margined paths,
yellow blossoms of wild black mustard spread
   over an unploughed field, release silent symbols.
A tamarind grove stands sentry over unmarked burials —
   centuries old.

Winds, nibbling canebrakes, ask the mute:
   why don't they talk about you?
A purple dragonfly escorts shadows
   to tufts in the flowers' centers.

COMMUNING WITH THE DEAD

Speared canebrakes guard the old farm.
   Whose grandmother shoots up calcium
into their veins?

Rice paddies emerald the flooded field
   older villages, swamped, soak stories
of a drowned bridegroom's struggle
   to hold back high water
in the rainy season.

Throats clogged with sand dried mud
   Swallow legends of endurance;
wet weeds curled around grasses
   bearing food grains full of tears
withered before the telling.

Do they wave in wild mustard
shooting from this barren field?

Memory — what is it?
   Silence ripens into weeds
daring yellow.

CAIMANS CROSSING

You rode ancient seas between
land masses, following swamp ,
flooded savannah, river, lake,
fish, birds, deer
served in lavish feasts.

Somehow you've transferred
survival to us — live well and thrive —
in Amazonian forest-towns
we build houses of wood and brick,
thundering rain turns white paint grey,
crawls under doors.

We're here on sufferance
but remain.

When at night you cross the asphalt,
we brake, watch our lights bounce
against black massive head and jaws,
glittering, before you slide
into cane fields under water.

We're kin,
carried by ancient seas
become slave-road between continents,
make the swamps our own,
leave spaces for you
master of nocturnal ways.

SEA CUCUMBERS

Down to the water's edge
           to bury my secret dead
shrouded in bark and leaves

discarded unwanted garments
           from tree and shrub
I sink them into caverns

deep beneath cross currents
           where river first meets ocean
where reed anemones spring their feelers

to sting shrimp inching through
           sea lavender, where sea cucumbers
move on suction-feet

mouths frilled to devour fish
           mistaking movements of soft purr
before they halve themselves to escape danger

as I split myself at this burial
           each cut end open
to the water's changes.

THE HIDDEN GOD

I

Columbus: *I do nothing but go forward to find gold*
      the forest slings its noose of fragrance.
Golden mask — chief's gift — can't quell his questing bite,
      between islands no longer spice-driven.

II

Raleigh: *I hold my soul in my teeth*
      crossing oceans three times gripped by *el dorado*,
king showered with gold dust.
      Imaginary monsters haunt his certainty of the scaffold.

III

Cortez: *In this land as much gold as Solomon took for the temple.*
      From Aztecs, a large gold wheel imprinted
with jaguar and maize stirs his hunger; gold bells
      bordering necklaces
      blue birds, eyes, beaks of gold — furnace bound.

IV

Their sails bellied into our reefs and bays. Intent?
      Shatter our gods,
while they worshiped Mammon, sought his shrines.
Rulers mutated into receivers of stolen goods.
      Cinnamon and pepper forgotten in gold's dazzle.

V

I hear echoes from the past in a field of grasses
      soaked in water from withered eyes;
bird song trills, secreted elegies carried on the wind.
      Marsh fractures into shards of bone.

MINUS A GODDESS

I could claim a goddess:
   Aphrodite through tutelage
trailing red cyclamen
from the Aegean
to the Antilles.

   Or Erzulie
robes scented with oils and cinnamon
to soothe wounds
inflicted when ships leaving Africa
advanced west.

   Or Amazon Orehu
river-dark hair
the water's crest
seed necklaces
over her nakedness.

   Their ceremonies escape me.
   Statues, museums
   try to explain them.

Prayer beads found in the flea market
have lost power to bring up
spirits long buried
beneath the scraps.

MORPHO TRAIL

Pinned in its case, a large blue butterfly kidnaps her speech.
    Preserved in formaldehyde, death's fluid,
it fuels desire for its natural quarters,
    progressions from egg to pupa to chrysalis.
What color its caterpillars? What leaves its feed?
    At home, her own eat sweet apples, pears, plums,
tulip bulb, *Semper Augustus*, one thousand florins.
    Maria Sibylla escapes such craziness

to Suriname: cabinet of living curiosities.
    On shore, malaria strikes. Heat, mosquitoes, frogs
cover river banks, floods. Collecting? Amerindians,
    enslaved Africans assist. They know the peacock plant,
abortion helper. White peacock caterpillars feed on cassava,
    sphinx moths on custard apples, genip, guava, papaya,
hang from trees like Indians in their hammocks, she writes
    from a land in sugar's shackles, tighter
        than Turkey's tulip.

I turn the pages of her masterwork on Suriname's insects,
    hunting a sketch of helpers, like Velazquez' Juan.
I'm defined by owl moth and boa. Her countrymen caterpillage
    the Indies, East and West, denuding landscapes
        efficiently.
She draws holes in leaves, their badge. People bring insects
    to her: musical, they whistle at night, assassins
on tree trunks. She can't wander the forest alone.
    Detailed banana, coveted morpho, sphinx moth
        show her skill.

She sees whip, lash, hog-tie; owns slaves. No break
          from her circle.
No children eat guavas or suffer from giant
          silkworm stings.
First gold. Then moths and ants.

NIGHT-BLOOMING CEREUS

Blooms on its cactus host
with vanilla scent
only in moonlight.

We invite friends, relatives
to witness the miracle.
Rice wine? Rum

to raise joy to the full moon,
and her acolyte?
Not an old religion.
not a heathen belief.

Its ceremonial opening
captures Margaret Mee.
To find. To draw.
To color in the Amazon

at night from a boat's deck.
By lantern light.

Here photography is kind.
Helpers, boatmen, native people
named: Mocinhu, Radiokuhi.

In our village
celebration along
the aqueduct.

VICTORY

Landing there revealed Eden,
Paradise, Fragrant lands.

People making gods
from the sweat of the sun
tears of the moon.

In botanic gardens, hard work
bring the tropical flowers north
to bloom in summer.

Reality? Forests, not woods;
giants whose leaves scrape sky.
Leaf, flower, scent impossible to capture.
Paint them. Own them

despite beauty's goodbyes.

Oh, for a wand to make people disappear!

The forest seduces, ensnares, its ways of life
rooted in rain and sun, trunk, and canopy,
reclaimed by downpours peculiar to itself.

We see them come and go,
our own disappearing
with them into other worlds.

We adapt, change, salute,
They rip and tear.
The forest sees, waits for the flood.

SECRET TEXTS

Crossing landscapes, from interwoven forests
to plains longing for distant horizons. I read
Inca geometric messages lodged
in surface story. Their power brings

canopy and river closer to concrete
through viridian threads:, white egrets
in pairs, species of butterflies
fish slant crosswise in a blue lake, clues

in dark chocolate trace a dried spine
beside sunflower yellow merged
with marigolds. Not a trophy plundered
from Peruvian graves to decorate museum walls

in Brooklyn or Goteburg provoking battles
across oceans. Spider Woman's heir breathes
among alpaca fibers, weaves her stitches;
tears and laughter idle in their crevices.

Cradling her loom, her lap bears new scripts.
If only I could read them.

Dolphin Dances

Myth — northerners seeking fame capture him in a name
    hear how enchanted Dolphins emerge from lakes,
their underground city gleams with gold; how they saunter
        into crowds
    at village dances, males in straw hats, white suits, new shoes,
seduce men and women, mate with them, produce children,
        disappear at dawn.
    You can see the lights from the shore.

Dance cards and tracks from shoes — ancient, visible —
    mark southern trails and paths through mountain
and forest. Dangled first lure: gold to Columbus, Cortez;
    silver tricks Pizarro. Change wove cloaks
to hide men in companies glued on bauxite bait.
    Latest taunt — oil leaving poisonous trails
unable to wipe out the cavorting creature's own.

Myth — intruders follow; Dolphin muddies their dreams
    as they scab mountain, scar forest seeking the golden city.

CELEBRATION

(Response to Sandburg's "Wilderness")

A spider monkey swings through
 the high canopy of my brain
he tells me when to hang-glide
or when to let go;
the jungle gives him to me.

An ocelot clenches his muscles in mine
his orange fur bulges with black roses;
the jungle's gift of the cat-mind;

the harpy eagle, slate-black with a white breast,
 arranges the lines of my face when I'm angry
and gives me her raptor's ferocity;
I raise my crest before I pounce.

The red-and-yellow macaw colors my dreams,
lingers in my half-awake morning,
gift in the dawn light
a shimmer before I open my eyes.

I have become an alligator
long snout and pebbled back,
hidden among crowds in packed buses,

watching for ways of a slither-escape.
I draw the hood over my eyes
to block out the subway's
menace.

I carry my animal-wealth
in my body's bag,
jungle gifts I will not let go.

About the Poems

Epigraphs are quotations for *The Journal of Christopher Columbus*, trans. Cecil Jane. Appendix R. A Skelton (New York: Clarkson N. Potter, Inc., 1960). Jane reminds readers that his translation is from the edition prepared by Bartolomé de las Casas (1484-1566), probably from a Barcelona copy. For details, see Cecil Jane's "Introduction."

First Whispers. "Creatures, like us, coming from sea caves." The Taino, who met Columbus, had an origin myth telling that humans emerged from caves. Arawak myth, on the other hand, stated that humans descended from the sky. See John Bierhorst, *The Mythology of South America* (New York: William Morrow, 1988, 65-66).

Cipangu. The name Columbus gave the place he was looking for; the names for the islands are what he understood the Taino to say since he did not speak their language.

Darning Needles. Guacanagari: Taino chief.

Meadow Hawk (1616). "I hold faste my soule in my teeth, till it were performed"— Raleigh's letter to Charles Howard and Robert Cecil on his determination to perform his task. *Destiny* is the name of his last ship. He was beheaded on charges of treason. *The Discoverie of the Large, Rich and Bewtiful Empyre of Guiana*. Trans, annotated, and intro. by Neil L. Whitehead (Norman: Univ. of Oklahoma Press, 1997, 121).

Explorer's Map. Abraham Ortelius (1527-1598) was a Flemish cartographer.

Zong Survivor's Psalm (1781). The *Zong* was a British slave ship at the heart of a great scandal. See James Walvin, *The Zong: a Massacre, the Law and the End of Slavery* (New Haven and London: Yale University Press, 2011).

Tituba: Flame Skimmer. Accused and imprisoned as a witch in the Salem Witch Trials (1692). No record has been found of her execution.

Sacrifice. The mummy of a young girl approximately 11-15 years old, killed between 1450 and 1480, was found frozen in the Peruvian Andes in 1995 by anthropologists Johan Reinhard and Miguel Zárate (*The Ice Maiden: Inca Mummies and Sacred Sites in the Andes*. Washington, D.C.: National Geographic, 2005).

Sugar's Trap. The Demerara River is found in Guyana, South America, and runs through several sugar estates.

Ticuna Response. The Ticuna are one of the most populous of Brazilian Amazonian peoples.

Self-Portrait. Greek poet Odysseus Elytis (1911-1996) won the Nobel prize in 1979.

The Craft of Erasure. Mahmoud Darwish, celebrated Palestinian poet (1941-2008). Louis-Antoine, Comte de Bougainville (1729-1811) sailed around the world, 1763-1764, accompanied by botanist Philibert Commerson (1727-1773). In Argentina, Commerson found the flowering shrub and named it after his commander. (John Dunmore, *Storms and Dreams: Louis de Bougainville: Soldier, Explorer, Statesman*. Gloucester: Nonsuch Publishing Ltd., 2005).

Cross Pollination. The British commandeered estates in India, some from maharajahs who owed them enormous sums, to grow the poppies, which became opium shipped to China. Two recent novels, *Sea of Poppies*, and *River of Smoke*, by Amitav Ghosh deal with this history.

Wandering Glider. Charles Plumier, (1646-1704), a French monk, was appointed royal botanist by Louis XIV and made three trips to the French Antilles collecting plants for Versailles.

Morpho Trail. Maria Sibylla Merian (1647-1717) was a German artist and scientist who moved to Amsterdam. In 1699 she traveled with her daughter Dorothea to Surinam to study insects in their tropical habitat. When she contracted malaria, she returned to Amsterdam with a large collection of watercolors and preserved insects. They were published as *Metamorphosis Insectorum Surinamensium* (Metamorphosis of the Insects of Surinam) in 1705. Introduction and notes by Katharina Schmidt Loske in English, German, and French (Basel: Taschen, n.d.). The book may also be found online at www.archive.org by searching its Latin title.

Night-Blooming Cereus. Margaret Mee (1909-1988) an English botanist, spent several years in the Brazilian Amazon, photographing its people, recording her helpers' names, and painting abundant flora in watercolors. *Margaret Mee's Amazon: Diaries of an Artist Explorer.* (Kew: The Royal Botanic Gardens, 2004).

Dolphin Dances. Amazonian folklore records experiences of people living in the rain forest who have danced with dolphins as humans who appear at village parties but return to dolphin-shape when they hit the lake's waters and return to their golden city under the lake. Candace Slater, *Dance of the Dolphin: Transformation and Disenchantment in the Amazonian Imagination* (Chicago and London: The University of Chicago Press, 1994).

About the Author

Jacqueline de Weever, born in Georgetown, British Guiana (now Guyana), was educated there and in New York, earning a Ph.D at the University of Pennsylvania. She is Professor Emerita at Brooklyn College, City University of New York, where she taught English Medieval Literature for 29 years. She has published four books in her field: *Chaucer Name Dictionary* (Garland, 1988); *Mythmaking and Metaphor in Black Women's Fiction* (St. Martin's Press, 1991); *Sheba's Daughters: Whitening and Demonizing the Saracen Woman in French Medieval Epic* (Garland, 1998); and *Aesop and the Imprint of Medieval Thought* (McFarland, 2011). Her poetry has been widely published in *Blue Unicorn, The Cape Rock Review, Sensations Magazine, Tiger's Eye, Tribeca Poetry Review, Vanitas*, among others. A resident of Brooklyn, she is also a watercolor painter.

About this Book

The body type for this book is Adobe Caslon Pro, a modern adaptation of a classic typeface that was brought to the American colonies by Benjamin Franklin. Font designer Carol Twombly based this digital version on various fonts by William Caslon used between 1734 and 1770. Poem titles are in Solemnis, an uncial typeface designed in 1953 by Günter Gerhard Lange for the Berthold Foundry.

The typeface used on the cover and title-page is Liffey Script.

The cover art is from an engraving in Maria Sibylla Merian's *Metamorphosis of the Insects of Surinam* (1705). The engraving of the caiman and snake is also from a painting by Merian. The wood engraving on page 12, "Oceanica Classis," is from the first edition of Columbus's *Letter to Sanchez,* printed in 1493 by Jakob Wolff, from the New York Public Library Digital Collections.

www.ingramcontent.com/pod-product-compliance
Lightning Source LLC
Chambersburg PA
CBHW051702040426
42446CB00009B/1253